AS Philosophy c

REVISION GUIDE

AS Level Religious Studies
Component 01

OCR B (H173, H573)

Matthew Livermore

AS Philosophy of Religion for OCR REVISION GUIDE

AS Religious Studies OCR specifications and past exam questions © OCR Examination Board, used with permission. References are included from the Oxford English Dictionary, some meanings are omitted, changed slightly or added to. Bible quotes refer to the New International Version.

ISBN: 978-1-78484-144-7 (pbk)
ISBN: 978-1-78484-147-8 (hbk)
ISBN: 978-1-78484-150-8 (ebk)
ISBN: 978-1-78484-153-9 (kin)

Published in the United Kingdom by PushMe Press.

www.pushmepress.com

In this module much of the foundation for the whole A Level is laid. The study of ancient philosophical influences in Plato and Aristotle's thought is properly basic to any understanding of religious philosophy, ethics and Christian thought. This is because these two philosophers have bequeathed an epistemology (theory of knowledge) and an ontology (study of existence/being) that has been profoundly influential on the development of Christian culture. In other words, Plato's theory of knowledge has moulded strands of thought within western culture that are still influential today in such spheres as education and aesthetics. Equally, Aristotle could be said to have been influential on everything from medicine to law.

The topics in the philosophy module reflect this:

- The idea of soul as opposed to body

- The classical arguments for God

- Religious experience

- The problem of evil

all reveal fundamental debates about the way we attain knowledge:

- What should be kept in or left out of a study of "reality"

- The nature of the human condition

- Whether faith can ever be a prerequisite for certain types of knowledge

- Whether there are rational or evidential arguments which can lead to knowledge of God

- Whether matter is all there is, or if 'matter' is other than what is currently understood by science

Simplistic religious notions of "soul" are challenged - what is this thing called soul and how is it supposed to interact with body?

But materialism is not let off the hook either - how can it give a coherent account of itself and avoid challenges that point out that it is based on a paradox? For instance if we are meant to believe in materialism, presumably that is because it is rationally worthy of belief - but given that for a materialist the "mind" is simply a "bunch of tricks" as Daniel Dennett calls it, questions arise about what it can possibly mean for such a phenomenon to rationally hold a belief.

How to use this book

The OCR Religious Studies AS offers a wide range of choice for the teacher and student to pick from. There are three one hour and fifteen minute exams: one Philosophy, one Ethics and one from a perspective of religious thought.

This book provides you with detailed summaries of all parts of the OCR AS Religious Studies Component 01 on Philosophy of Religion specification.

We have put extra resources on our website which you can access by scanning the code at the end of the chapter with your smartphone. The website resources are also organised under the specification headings. The code will take you directly to the module you have scanned and you can browse between modules on the site. You will find Key Quotes, Practice Questions and more. If you are reading a Kindle version of this book, you can click on the link at the end of each chapter.

At the beginning of each chapter, you will find a list of key words and their definitions. Many of these key words are in **BOLD** in the text so that you can see them used in context. In places, other words are highlighted as prompts for you to remember the content.

Contents

Philosophical Language and Thought

Plato

Death & the Afterlife

THE FORMS

Plato

Plato (428-348 BC) was a philosopher in ancient Greece, whose teacher was Socrates and whose pupil was Aristotle. He has had a profound influence on the development of Western Thought, so much so that A N Whitehead, in his "Process and Reality", has said that:

> *"The safest general characterization of the European philosophical tradition is that it consists of a series of footnotes to Plato."*

The focus here is on Plato's **THEORY OF KNOWLEDGE**, which is a branch of philosophy called **EPISTEMOLOGY**. Such questions as what constitutes knowledge, belief and opinion, how we are justified in holding something to be true, and the relationship between morality and knowledge are at the heart of this chapter.

KEYWORDS

- **FORMS** - The essence or idea of something which is universal and non-spatial, and which is prior to a particular thing, eg. The Form of Triangle is the true triangle, of which all actual triangles drawn on paper or anywhere else are mere copies

- **FORM OF BEAUTY** - The essence or idea of beauty, not itself a beautiful thing

- **PARTICULAR** - An individual object, which has existence in relation to its Form

- **KNOWLEDGE** - Justified true belief

- **OPINION** - Knowledge of particulars, a mixture of truth and falsity

- **EPISTEME** - Greek for knowledge

- **DOXA** - Greek for opinion

- **ANALOGY OF THE CAVE** - Plato's story to illustrate the difference between the World of Forms and world of particulars

- **INTELLIGIBLE** - Capable of direct intuition without need for discursive reason - knowable through the intellect

- **SENSIBLE** - Capable of being experienced through the senses

- **RATIONALISM** - Belief in supremacy of reason and a priori knowledge over empirical methods of knowing

- **EMPIRICISM** - Belief that all knowledge is based on experience acquired through the senses

PLATO'S UNDERSTANDING OF REALITY

Plato's reliance on reason rather than the senses

Plato's understanding of reality is formed by his interpretation of pre-Socratic debates about the nature of the world. In particular he sets out to answer questions about the possibility of knowledge when everything is changing, and therefore has no permanent essential self. He also tries to answer questions related to **THE ONE AND THE MANY** - ie. if there was only really one thing, or if there were many things. To us these seem odd questions, but they form the basis of a theory of knowledge which is still influential today.

Plato's quest

How can we have knowledge of changing things?

HERACLITUS (a pre-Socratic philosopher) said **PANTA RHEA** - everything flows - in other words there is no abiding essence to anything. Plato was working in the shadow of this problem.

Why was it a problem? Because if I know something is a certain way, but that thing changes, I can no longer be said to have knowledge of that thing. Even more basic than this is that if everything is changing, then nothing has an essence - the very notion of essence relies on the fact that there is an unchanging core of something - and if nothing has an essence then nothing is really knowable.

Take as an example the difference between knowing that the interior angles of a triangle add up to 180 degrees, and knowing that Burford Brown chicken eggs have slightly more orange yolks than other eggs. My certainty about the first proposition is far greater - indeed it is as great as it is likely to ever be - and not because everyone says that the interior angles of a triangle add up to 180 degrees. It is because if I investigate I will be able to see that from the very nature of angles and triangles, it is impossible that it could not be true. Whereas, although my experience tells me that all the Burford Brown eggs I've seen in the past have had more orange yolks, that may not be the case for all Burford Brown eggs, or ones I may see in future.

MATHEMATICAL KNOWLEDGE is really analogous to the kind of knowledge that Plato requires in order to truly know anything. Plato argues that even though everything is changing, and that most of the time when we think we know something, we really don't - we have an opinion which is not the same thing. There is still the possibility of **TRUE KNOWLEDGE**. If there wasn't, it wouldn't even be possible to have an opinion about something, because to have an opinion is to be right in some ways and wrong in others. In other words, opinion only makes sense against a background of knowledge about what is actually the case.

What are these elements of true knowledge, which are not mere opinion, and are completely certain? They are called by Plato **THE FORMS**.

Plato's argument for what he calls the **FORMS** can be summarised in the following way:

- **PARTICULAR** - All things experienced through the senses are particular things

- **WE NEVER SENSE ABSTRACTS** - We can sense a beautiful rose but not beauty itself

- **BEAUTY** - Many things can be beautiful, so beauty is a property they share, so there must be something called beauty which can be shared by different things, even though not accessible through senses

- **FORM** - This universal idea of beauty is an example of what Plato called a Form

- **FORM OF BEAUTY** - For Plato, the form of beauty manifests itself in different particulars, eg. a rose, a face, or a sunset

- **DISTINCT** - But why should there be something called "the Form of Beauty" which is separate from particular beautiful things?

- **INDESTRUCTIBLE** - Because if you destroyed all beautiful things you would not destroy "beauty"

- **INDEPENDENT** - So particular beautiful things participate in the form of Beauty, but it is independent of them

THE NATURE OF KNOWLEDGE IN SUPPORTING THE THEORY OF FORMS

Analysis of knowledge gives more support to Plato's separation of particulars from Forms. **PARTICULARS** are always a mixture of properties. Therefore, a ball will partake of the form of roundness, shininess, blue-ness etc.

Particulars are also only relative to what they are. For example, something may be big, shiny or round but only relative to other (perhaps) bigger, shinier and rounder things. This means that our knowledge of any particular thing will always be **BOTH X** and **NOT-X**. In other words it will both be shiny and yet not shiny when compared with something shinier.

However, if particulars are only relatively shiny, large or round, then we cannot have true knowledge of particulars. Why? Because knowledge can only be of what is, never of what is not - you cannot know what is not true.

If something both is x and is not-x we cannot have knowledge of it

There is nothing beautiful that does not sometimes seem ugly, or seem ugly to some, or is only beautiful for a short time, but that means that it is, in some sense, both beautiful and not-beautiful.

But as we said before, you cannot have knowledge of what is not, so there must be another faculty at work when people disagree about the beautiful thing. Of course, that is opinion;

Plato argues knowledge and opinion (or **EPISTEME** and **DOXA**) are two different faculties.

Why? Because opinion can be mistaken but knowledge cannot: **YOU CANNOT KNOW WHAT IS FALSE**.

And as knowledge is about what is real, but ignorance is about what is not real, ie. does not exist (because if you are ignorant about something you know nothing of it at all), but knowledge of particulars seems to be somewhere in the middle of these two states (both x and not-x) then there should be a faculty somewhere in the middle.

This faculty is **OPINION**: It is not knowledge because it can be mistaken (see above), but it is not ignorance either, because you cannot have an opinion about nothing, opinion is always about something. Therefore, Plato argues that knowledge relates to the world of Forms and opinion relates to the world of senses. This means that the Forms must exist separately from the particulars.

THE NATURE & HIERARCHY OF THE FORMS

The Forms have certain fundamental properties:

- **SIMPLICITY** - The Forms are "one" - they only have the one property - eg the Form of Beauty is only beautiful. If they did not have this unity the forms would become particulars because they would become mixtures of properties

- **PERMANENCE** - Forms are unchanging. If they could change then that means they have become what they are or will become something else, which is clearly impossible as they either would not previously have been beautiful, or are not beautiful yet, which is a contradiction

- **PERFECTION** - Forms are the perfect examples - they are the standard by which the particular things which contain them are judged - if they were less than perfect they would not be the Form

- **SEPARATENESS FROM PARTICULARS** - Because of all of the above, Forms do not exist in time and space, and neither do they need to be manifested in particulars - they are the essence of themselves, in contrast to particulars which participate in these essences, but are not them

- **LOGICAL PRIORITY** - The Forms are what they are in virtue of themselves, whereas the particulars are what they are in virtue of the forms. Therefore, the Forms are logically prior to the particulars - the particulars are dependent on the Forms, which means there is a hierarchy, with the Forms at the top and the particulars further down

- **THE GOOD AS THE SUPREME FORM** - Just as the Forms are logically prior to the particulars, so the **FORM OF THE GOOD** is logically prior to the other Forms, because it is by this Form that all the other Forms are capable of being known; thus, the Form of Good is the Form of Forms. This is because the Forms of Beauty, Justice, Truth etc. are all themselves good, so they must in some sense participate in the Form of the Good, and the Good is at the basis of being able to know the Forms of Beauty or Justice or Truth

THE ANALOGY OF THE CAVE

The **ANALOGY OF THE CAVE** shows the journey that the philosopher makes from illusion to reality - from ignorance to the world of Forms.

A prisoner is chained alongside others facing a wall. Behind them is a fire and in front of that a raised wall, upon which objects are placed so that they cast their shadows onto the wall in front of the prisoners. One of the prisoners is freed, and first sees the fire, the objects and then begins the difficult ascent out of the cave. When he gets outside and his eyes become accustomed to the light he sees reflections of the moon and stars in water, then he sees them in the sky. Finally he sees the sun. When he returns to free the prisoners from the cave and tell them of the outside world they think he is mad and drive him away.

Each stage of the analogy has a meaning. They are:

- **THE CAVE** - The world of the senses

- **THE SHADOWS ON THE WALL** - Illusions: What we see and mistake for reality

- **THE CHAINS** - Ignorance

- **THE FIRE** - The sun

- **THE OBJECTS ON THE WALL** - Physical things

- **THE DIFFICULT ASCENT** - The dialectic – the process of arriving at truth

- **THE REFLECTIONS** - The process of understanding

- **THE MOON & STARS** - The Forms of justice, beauty etc.

- **THE SUN** - The Form of the Good

The purpose of the analogy and its relation to the theory of Forms

For **SOCRATES**, the teacher of Plato, education is not giving knowledge to those who lack it. That would be analogous to putting sight into blind eyes. It is rather turning the whole body and therefore the eye towards the light.

> "But then, if I am right, certain professors of education must be wrong when they say that they can put a knowledge into the soul which was not there before, like sight into blind eyes.
>
> They undoubtedly say this, he replied.
>
> Whereas our argument shows that the power and capacity of learning exists in the soul already; and that just as the eye was unable to turn from darkness to light without the whole body, so too the instrument of knowledge can only by the movement of the whole soul be turned from the world of becoming into that of being, and learn by degrees to endure the sight of being and of the brightest and best of being, or in other words, of the good."

Plato, The Republic, Book VII

The analogy illustrates important elements of Plato's theory:

▸ **Knowledge is remembering**

The effort needs to come from the individual to turn towards what is and away from what is not.

▸ **The whole soul should be turned to the light**

Education is not an intellectual exercise but a moral and spiritual conversion. This can be seen in the fact that the sun in the analogy reveals what exists by its light, just as we only know truly by the Form of the Good, all knowledge then has a moral dimension.

▸ **The intelligible world and the sensible world are related**

The latter is a shadow of the former. Just as the fire in the cave represents the sun in our physical world, so the sun in the analogy represents the Good, that by which everything which is, is made visible. Equally, we should take this as a prompt: Our sun, that by which we see, can only show us visible objects. We realise from the analogy that if our knowledge only extends to what we can see then we are stuck in the cave looking at the objects by the light of the fire.

This shows Plato's insistence that **RATIONALISM** is superior to **EMPIRICISM**.

EVALUATION OF PLATO'S THEORY OF FORMS AND CAVE ANALOGY

Do we need a separate "World of Forms" to explain how we can know anything?

Plato's theory in summary:

▸ **A theory of two worlds**

This is known as dualism.

▸ **Forms are one over many**

Whenever at least two things have something in common, the property they share in common is a Form.

▸ **Forms are paradigms**

Patterns or models on which things are dependent.

▸ **Things or particulars participate**

"There are certain forms, whose names these other things have through getting a share of them - as, for instance, they come to be like by getting a share of likeness, large by getting a share of largeness, and just and beautiful by getting a share of justice and beauty."

Phaedo, 130e-131a

Which means they are knowable on this basis:

- **GRASPED BY INTELLECT** - Knowledge of a particular, such as a vase, is not true knowledge, because the true vase is not known through the senses but rather grasped with the intellect

- **THE WORLD OF FORMS** - Contains all the non-spatial Forms which are behind the particulars - these Forms are distinguishable from the particulars in the same way that being is distinguished from becoming. The Forms actually exist, whereas the particulars only partially exist.

- **THE IDEAL STANDARD** - Without Forms as an ideal standard we would have nothing to appeal to when we make judgements - we implicitly assume the existence of the Form of Justice whenever we say that some particular thing is unjust, or more or less just than another thing.

Plato moves from some fairly innocuous initial observations to some rather drastic conclusions. Most philosophers agree that many of Plato's arguments for Forms are flawed and cannot offer support to his theory. However, it is often difficult to say exactly where the arguments are lacking, and students sometimes resort to saying "Plato has no evidence for his theory", which is partly understandable, but which on its own is just not adequate as criticism. Below I have tried to set out some of the major problems with the theory.

Evaluation

- **ONE OVER MANY IS NOT AN ARGUMENT** - "One Over Many" is not strictly an argument for the Forms. All it proves is that there are properties of things. Those properties might be **IMMANENT** - in this world, or they might simply be names we give to things - this is known as **NOMINALISM**.

- **THE THIRD MAN ARGUMENT** - Aristotle showed that the theory of Forms was subject to a criticism which reduced it to absurdity. If we have a collection of large things and their form "largeness" then we should consider the collection of things large, as well as the form "largeness" itself large. But in that case do we not have to appeal to a further form in order to consider largeness large? And why should we stop there?

  This criticism undermines the idea that the Forms can be ideal standards, by showing that we would need to appeal to an infinite amount of Forms simply to make one judgement.

- **LACK OF EMPIRICAL SUPPORT** - It is not really surprising that Plato provides little empirical evidence for his theory, as he shows, especially in the analogy of the Cave, that he believes empirical data is next to useless in gaining real knowledge. Plato is a rationalist, and as such makes use of logic and A PRIORI reasoning for his proofs.

- **PRACTICAL EFFECTIVENESS OF SCIENCE** - However, from a modern standpoint, it looks suspicious that the theory has so little grounding in empirical data, and indeed, appears completely counter-intuitive. For instance, if this world is not really real, and the World of Forms is invisible and only knowable through the intellect, how is it that we are able to predict the behaviour of this world so well through scientific theories? And not just predict but also manipulate and make the natural world work for us through the use of technology? If it is all an illusion, should it be capable of producing such practical beneficial outcomes for us as medicine etc.?

- **GUESSING GAMES** - It is worth bearing in mind that Plato was not able to see the astounding success of science which would come nearly 1800 years after his death, but it is possible that even if he could have foreseen it he might still have pointed to the prisoners making guesses about the objects that threw their shadows on the wall in his Cave analogy and implied that science is still just a really sophisticated version of this game. For Plato, truth was never decided on the principle of practical effectiveness which many point to to assert the importance of science.

NEED MORE HELP ON PLATO?

Use your phone to scan this QR code

Aristotle

Aristotle (384-322BC) was a Greek philosopher who, alongside Plato has had a profound effect on western thought. His works have been influential in Law, Medicine, Botany, Theology, Physics, Ethics and many other areas. Thomas Aquinas was so indebted to him that he called him simply "The Philosopher". In this chapter we will see how his ideas about cause, and what makes something what it is have led to theories about the universe, human beings, and their purpose.

KEYWORDS

- **AITION** - Greek word translatable as "because" - cause or reason for something

- **CAUSE** - Explanatory principle for something's existence

- **EXPLANATION** - Reason or reasons given for why something is as it is

- **POTENTIALITY** - Possibility of being something

- **ACTUALITY** - The state of something's being what it is meant to be

- **ACTUALISATION** - Process by which a thing becomes what it is meant to be

- **POTENCY** - The ability something has to become something

- **ACT** - Something's existence as opposed to its potency

- **AGENT** - Actor, thing which is the cause of something else

- **EFFICIENT CAUSE** - The "how" of something

- **MATERIAL CAUSE** - The "what" of something - the matter it is made from

- **FORMAL CAUSE** - The characteristics or blueprint of something

- **FINAL CAUSE** - The "why" of something - what it is for

- **TELEOLOGY** - Explanation of something in relation to ends or goals

- **LATENT** - Unrevealed, lying hidden in something

- **PRIME MOVER** - Unchanging first cause or principle behind the change we see in everything

- **A PRIORI** - Relating to knowledge which proceeds from theoretical reasoning rather than empirical data

ARISTOTLE'S VIEWS IN RELATION TO HIS UNDERSTANDING OF REALITY

ARISTOTLE considered at the beginning of his Physics that we can only know something inasmuch as we can explain it,

"Knowledge is the object of our inquiry, and men do not think they know a thing till they have grasped the 'why' of it"

For Aristotle, the word he used for the "why" of something was **AITION**, which has been translated as **CAUSE**, although **EXPLANATION** could also be used.

Aristotle draws a distinction between **POTENTIALITY** and **ACTUALITY**.

He applies this to the process of change (or motion). Change is simply the process by which an object acquires a new form (very different from Plato's idea of form). The object has the **POTENTIALITY** to become something different, and change is the **ACTUALISATION** of the potential of one form of matter to become another form of matter. For example, the block of marble has the potential to become an actual statue. The statue is **LATENT** within the block of marble - the block of marble has the capacity to become a statue.

There are two important things to note:

- **POTENCY** and **ACT** are distinct; the marble cannot be both a block and the statue at the same time. In another example a piece of wood cannot be both potentially on fire and actually on fire at the same time therefore, change is this movement between potential and actual.

- As the object cannot be both simultaneously potential and actual, how does it move from one to the other? Aristotle says it needs an **AGENT** to move it, which he called the **EFFICIENT CAUSE**. This must in itself be in a state of actuality, not potentiality, ie. it must exist to be a cause of the change in the object.

  For example, you need actual water to effect the change of an acorn into an oak tree.

THE FOUR CAUSES

So because of these two principles - firstly that of the distinction between potency and act, and secondly that there need to be actual things to move potential things, Aristotle is able to derive his theory of the four causes. We can see how from this Aristotle got the first two of his causes:

- **FIRST CAUSE (MATERIAL)** - There must be matter which undergoes the change from one form to another, so in one sense, if we say "what is it?" of something or ask for an explanation of it we can say what it is made of. For example, the statue is made of marble: This would be then the material cause.

- **SECOND CAUSE (EFFICIENT)** - There must also be other actual things which are able to act upon that material and move it from potential to actual itself. These are the efficient causes. In the case of the block of marble it would be the sculptor with his chisel.

But Aristotle did not believe we could stop with just the material and efficient causes, the what and the how, as you might say. He believed that as the material has undergone a change of form in going from a potential thing to an actual thing, that part of its explanation was what the characteristics of it were. If we were to say to a person "what makes you the person you are?" they would normally not give a straight list of the elements that compose them such as carbon - they would probably talk about their upbringing or give a character trait, such as "I'm happy-go-lucky". Therefore we need to add another cause other than the purely material to get at a full explanation of a thing - we need to talk about its characteristics. For example, a chair is more than just some wood, it is an object with four legs and a space to sit.

- **THIRD CAUSE (FORMAL)** - In the statue example the formal cause would be its particular qualities of marble sculpted into the form of a body, head etc. The formal cause of something is the FORM of the thing - the pattern which makes it what it is - in the case of a building it would be the blueprint. This is not as easily understandable as the other causes, and has been seen as slightly controversial. Clearly, though, much debate surrounds the notion of a form and many agree that Aristotle's notion is no less flawed than Plato's.

- **FOURTH CAUSE (FINAL)** - This comes from the end of a thing, what it is for. This idea of a purposive cause is given by Aristotle because something's aim or goal is also an important part of an explanation of the thing. Aristotle gives the example of the final cause of walking, medicine, purging, surgical instruments etc. as all being for health. In the example of the statue, the final cause of the statue is for decoration or to give aesthetic pleasure. For Aristotle the aim of something can be seen as its greatest good, this is brought out in our use of language when we ask of an object "what is it good for?"

Aristotle's use of teleology

This emphasis on the telos, or the goal of something is a key part of Aristotle's thought. We remember that for Aristotle change is the actualisation of something's potential, with respect to its potentiality. In other words, something can only become what it has it in it to be - so a lump of wood can become a bed, or a block of marble a statue, but a piece of iron cannot become a wombat, nor can a human become a bird. The potential of something may be latent until something else acts upon it, but if that thing acts upon it in a directed manner and brings about its potential, then we can speak of the telos of something being achieved.

Modern science focuses on the efficient cause, when explaining the physical world, and in fact, the final cause is not considered. Of course, when we are talking of the human world, it makes sense to talk about why something happened in terms of a final cause. Some examples:

Why did John stay in last night rather than go to Mary's party? He wanted to avoid seeing Jane whom he dislikes.

Why did you make that cake for Peter? I wanted to cheer him up.

These are teleological reasons; They make sense in terms of what goal someone had in mind, and as such we would not get a very good understanding of those actions if we left them out.

THE PRIME MOVER

The **PRIME MOVER** is the logical outcome of the theory of four causes. If everything is moving from a state of potentiality to actuality, but everything potential requires something else actual to move it, then unless you posit some kind of unmoved mover, then you do not have a sufficient explanation for the movement of the whole series of things, or so Aristotle argues, because you cannot keep going back forever in a series of moved things, or you would never have a reason for the movement you currently observe.

You might notice that the argument for the Prime Mover is essentially the same as the **COSMOLOGICAL ARGUMENT** for God, which you will look at in the next module. The Prime Mover is an absolute, and has many similar characteristics to the Christian notion of God, but the two are not the same. In the same way that Plato's Form of the Good, is not really the same as God, even though it seems to fulfill a similar function, the same applies to the Prime Mover.

Another way of looking at the Prime Mover is from the standpoint of **FINAL CAUSE**. If everything has a reason or goal for its existence, then it could be said that the Prime Mover is the **ULTIMATE GOAL** of the whole collection of things called the **UNIVERSE**.

In summary then:

- **LOGICAL RESULT** - The Prime Mover is a logical result of the application of final cause to the whole universe

- **PURE ACTUALITY** - It attracts all to itself as the end or goal of all - there is no potentiality in it at all. It is pure actuality

- **CHANGE HAPPENS** - Remember the movement from potentiality to actuality is going on in all things – that is another way of saying that change is happening to them

- **SOME THINGS DON'T CHANGE** - Most things are changing (being generated and being destroyed) but some things are not changing in that way. Aristotle thinks here of the heavenly spheres, containing the planets and fixed stars, and which were considered to be nested around each other about the earth

- **CYCLICAL MOTION** - These are only undergoing change in the sense of cyclical motion, and are not (according to Aristotle) being generated or destroyed

- **MOVEMENT IS REALITY** - This is because their movement is the reality behind time itself, and for Aristotle time cannot be destructible. It is uniform and everlasting

- **MOVEMENT OF THE SPHERES** - The movement of the spheres causes the change in the universe. Each sphere causes the one inside it to move, until you get to the outermost sphere, which has to be moved by something which is not itself moved (or it would need an explanation for its own movement). This is called the **PRIMUM MOBILE** or the **PRIME MOVER**

- **CAUSE OF MOTION** - The object of desire moves other things without itself moving (think of how a saucer of milk draws a cat to it). In this way the prime mover is the cause of the motion of all other things

- **FINAL NOT EFFICIENT CAUSE** - The Prime Mover is immaterial and is the teleological cause of the universe

- **DRAWN IN** - All things are being drawn to it, as to their own final end

- **IMMUTABLE** - The Prime Mover is unchanging and unaffected by anything

- **CONSEQUENCES OF IMMUTABILITY** - Because of its immutability it is therefore everlasting, impassive and necessary

Evaluation of the Prime Mover

The Aristotelian idea of the Prime Mover profoundly affected the notion of God that the Church developed. In particular scholastic theologians such as Aquinas blended scripture with Aristotle and Plato's ideas of God, and arrived at an immutable, impassible, eternal, immaterial and necessary being. The problem is that there is a great tension between the God of scripture and the God of philosophy. Some problems:

- If God is immutable then why bother praying to Him?

- If God is unaware and unaffected by the world, what do we make of the scriptural passages in which He takes an active interest in the world

- If God is unaware of the world, then how can He know everything that will happen (omniscience)?

Some answers might be:

- Prayer does not change God, it changes the one praying

- God in Himself is unchanging, but through his immanent aspect (the Logos or Spirit) he takes an interest in all things

- God is not the same thing as the Prime Mover - Aquinas makes crucial adjustments to the idea to fit with scripture. Eg. For Aristotle God is pure Being, but for Aquinas what this essentially means is pure overflowing love - all being is being-for-another, and the relationship of God in the Trinity cannot be reduced to Aristotelian ideas

- In other words Greek philosophy alone is insufficient for an understanding of God - we need revelation and especially the Trinitarian revelation that we find throughout scripture

The Prime Mover versus The Form of the Good

▶ Similarities

- **BOTH LINKED** - Both are linked in the domain of ethics. The Prime Mover through the idea of everything being drawn to its own purpose, and the form of the Good as the means by which everything that exists is known

- **BOTH ULTIMATES** - They are both "ultimates" which might appeal to non-theistic deists - impersonal sources of reality, arrived at through philosophical speculation, rather than faith

- **BOTH EXEMPLARS** - They have both served as exemplars for a way of explaining the world in terms of a "theory of everything" - arguably without them, science as we know it could not have developed

▶ Differences

- **ARGUMENTS** - The Prime Mover is based on arguments that appeal to **A POSTERIORI** evidence, the form of the Good on A PRIORI arguments

- **IMMANENT** - The Prime Mover is immanent - ie. within the world, whereas the Form of the Good is **NON-SPATIAL** and **NON-TEMPORAL**

- **MORE EXPLANATORY** - The Prime Mover has more explanatory power than the Form of the Good, which is posited as the source of all good things

Rationalism or Empiricism?

- **SENSES** - How dependent on our senses are we for knowledge? How you answer this question will largely form your assumptions about rationalism and empiricism.

- **EMPIRICAL SUPERIORITY** - Empiricists argue that sense experience is the ultimate source of knowledge. They have heavy intuitive support for this from our everyday experience - we know that we rely to a great deal on our senses to get around

- **INDEPENDENT CONCEPTS** - However, rationalists argue that concepts are independent of sense-experience, in that no matter how much sense-data you have, that can never in itself constitute knowledge - some kind of analytical function has to occur, which is not in itself simply the accumulation of more data

- **EPISTEMOLOGICAL** - Therefore it is a debate in the field of epistemology (philosophy of knowledge)

- **SCEPTICISM** - **HUME** (empiricist) said that ideas do not exist in themselves independently from objects, other than as a relation between objects. For instance, see Hume's Fork

However, there are good arguments for the existence of non-empirical rational objects, for instance the argument from ontological commitment, which might reinforce rationalist or Platonic arguments.

NEED MORE HELP ON ARISTOTLE?

Use your phone to scan this QR code

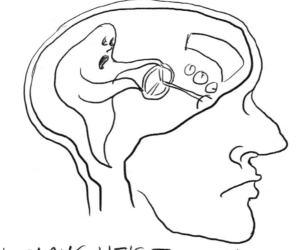

THE GHOST IN THE MACHINE

LEARNS HE'S JUST A CATEGORY ERROR

The Nature of Soul, Mind and Body

In this chapter we will examine different views on identity, awareness and the nature of mind. In particular we will look at the different arguments people have given for a belief in a non-material substance (sometimes called mind or soul) as well as a material substance (body). Some philosophers have argued that the concept of a non-material substance is incoherent, and that the facts can be explained by a monist materialist view (that there is only one substance which is matter, and that mind is ultimately based on this).

KEYWORDS

- **WILL** - Faculty of self-determination, ability to direct one's self as one wishes

- **APPETITE** - Desires or passions

- **REASON** - Faculty of cognition including power to think and form judgements logically

- **BLUEPRINT** - Master plan or overview - template

- **DUALISM** - Belief in two substances

- **MONISM** - Belief in one substance

- **MECHANISTIC** - Describing explanations which argue in reductive or materialistic terms

- **MATERIALISM** - Belief that reality is composed of the one substance of matter

- **EXTENSION** - Spreading-out in space

- **CARTESIAN DUALISM** - Term for Descartes' type of substance dualism

- **EMPIRICAL** - Reasoning based on data gathered from sense experience

- **GHOST IN THE MACHINE** - Ryle's term for the category mistake of assuming non-material explanations for objects which can be explained in material/behavioural terms

- **CATEGORY MISTAKE** - An error of thinking

- **PHILOSOPHICAL BEHAVIOURISM** - A theory of mind that mental concepts can be explained in terms of behavioral concepts

- **QUALIA** - A quality as experienced by a person, eg. the smell of fresh-baked bread

- **INTENTIONALITY** - The quality of mental states which consists in their being directed towards some object or state of affair

- **CONSCIOUSNESS** - State or quality of awareness

- **ROMANTICISM** - Movement in literature and the arts which rejected enlightenment rationalism and emphasised inspiration and subjectivity

PLATO'S VIEW OF THE SOUL

From the **ANALOGY OF THE CAVE** and the **THEORY OF FORMS** it can be seen that for Plato the soul is a non-material essence.

The **CHARIOTEER ANALOGY** helps to understand the tripartite (threefold) nature of the soul: Two horses (**WILL** and **APPETITE**) are controlled by the charioteer (**REASON**). Plato believed that unless the charioteer keeps control on the reins, the will (the weaker horse) will be dragged in the direction that the appetite (the stronger horse) wants to go.

Plato was a **DUALIST** and believed that the soul is deformed through its association with the body. The soul is separable from the body, and as it is non-material, is in a sense indestructible

PLATO'S ARGUMENTS FOR THE SOUL

- **THE CYCLICAL NATURE OF EXISTENCE** - As sleep follows waking, so waking follows sleep, and as death follows life, so life follows death

- **THE ARGUMENT FROM KNOWLEDGE** - Plato claims we have innate knowledge by which to make comparisons, which can only come from the world of the Forms – therefore our souls pre-existed our physical bodies in this world

Since it is the soul and not the body that grasps the Forms, then the soul must belong to that world too. In that case it is unchangeable and indivisible, just as the Forms are.

ARISTOTLE'S VIEW OF THE SOUL

Aristotle had an entirely different view of the soul. The soul is the **FORM OF THE BODY**.

For Aristotle, the form of something is related to the cause, specifically the formal cause, which is the **BLUEPRINT** or map of something.

The form of something is found in its functioning

The form of the car, for example, is found through the combustion of petrol, the action of the engine and the movement of the wheels. In other words, the working-together of all the processes of the car.

In that sense, you cannot say that you have a BMW if all you have is a pile of BMW parts: They have to be connected together and functioning in the manner intended.

Equally, even if you have a collection of human parts, unless they all function together you cannot say that there is a soul or form of human there.

The soul is inseparable from the body

It follows from the above that, in contrast to Plato's dualist position, Aristotle does not hold that the soul is separable from the body - that when the body dies, you cannot meaningfully speak of a form or soul of the body because decomposition begins.

An analogy to this is that of the eye - Aristotle says the soul of the eye is the sight. If the eye is not functioning there is no sight, and equally if the body is not functioning there is no soul.

Or another way Aristotle gives is the wax and the seal. When heated wax is imprinted with someone's seal or stamp (to seal an official letter for instance) it is impossible to separate the imprint of the seal from the wax itself. In this way the form of the body, the soul, is imprinted on it, but is also inseparable from the working of the body itself.

METAPHYSICS OF CONSCIOUSNESS

Descartes' Substance Dualism

Descartes' (1596-1650) was a French philosopher, mathematician and scientist who has had a major influence on western thought. He arrived at his position on the soul as a result of a profound scepticism about what it was possible to know. He is famous for his thought experiment:

- **DEMON DECEPTION** - An evil demon deceives you into believing that the evidence of your senses is real, but in fact it is entirely illusory

- **CANNOT BE CERTAIN** - How do you know for sure that this is not the case? The point is that you cannot entirely be certain that this is not true

- **THERE MUST BE A YOU** - However, even if you assume that there is a deceiver, it follows from the fact of you being deceived that there is a "you" - that much is certain

- **THINKING IS REAL** - Whilst you can be deceived about the content of thoughts (eg. that there is a world which is presented to your senses), you cannot be deceived that you are a thinking subject that seems to perceive things

In other words, there needs to be a subject - **YOU** - who is the subject of the deception.

Descartes frames this as **COGITO ERGO SUM** or;

"I think therefore I am"

So we can have certainty that there is a mental substance or "thinking", and we can be sure that that is not the same as matter. How can we be sure of this?

By application of **LEIBNIZ' LAW OF IDENTITY** (if two things are the same thing they must share all the same properties)

The argument here goes:

- **I CAN BE SURE THAT MY MIND EXISTS** - See the evil demon experiment

- **I CANNOT BE SURE THAT MY BODY EXISTS** - See above, again

- **MIND AND BODY MUST BE TWO SEPARATE SUBSTANCES** - By application of Leibniz' Law, they must be two separate substances because, if they were the same thing we would be able to be certain the body existed as well

So Descartes has arrived at the conclusion that mind and body are not the same thing. In fact, Descartes says that the key difference is that matter (body) is extended in space (he calls it **RES EXTENSA**) and mind is unextended (he calls it **RES COGITANS**).

This echoes Plato's earlier dualism in which the soul (mind) is essentially non-material and indivisible.

Evaluation

▸ Weaknesses

- **MAJOR FLAWS** - There are major flaws with Descartes' theory. Firstly, he fails to give a coherent account of how mind and body interact, when one is physical and spatial and the other non-physical and non-spatial.

- **PINEAL GLAND** - Descartes claimed that the two interacted via the pineal gland in the brain, but this is speculative

- **FROM WITHIN** - As we will see, Leibniz' law is not necessarily applicable to the difference between mind and body, as it may be that the supposed difference in properties is the result of viewing our consciousness from within (see next point)

- **MASKED MAN FALLACY** - Descartes' use of Leibniz' Law of Identity unfortunately falls foul of the Masked Man fallacy - If you saw a masked man at a party, and someone told you it was your father, if your response was 'that can't be my father; it looks nothing like him' then you would be making a major mistake. The same thing applies to Descartes' argument - he has not shown that mind and body actually have different properties, only that his perception of their properties differs in each case

- **CARTESIAN DUALISM** is Platonic in a sense as it is dualist, but the moral dimension of Plato's dualism has been lost - Descartes' dualism is **MECHANISTIC** - matter becomes nothing more than extension in space, and soul becomes pure spirit, devoid of any ethical character. This paves the way for the manipulation of physical forces by science and technology, and is a step on the road to the **DISENCHANTMENT** of the modern world where atheistic positivism holds sway.

▸ Strengths

- **SUBSTANCE DUALISM EASIER TO EXPLAIN** - Substance dualism does account for some features of consciousness that materialism finds difficult to explain:

- **QUALIA** - Qualities as experienced are one of these features. The problem of accounting for qualia is called by David Chalmers the "hard problem of consciousness"

- **EXPLANATORY GAP** - That is, why does the experience of the smell of fresh-cut grass have the form that it does, and not some other? Even if we can trace the chemicals which create the smell, we are no closer to explaining why it smells the way it does - this is known as the explanatory gap

- **DUALISM & DESCARTES** - We will see that such properties, inasmuch as they make materialism less plausible, provide support for dualism, and thus Descartes

MATERIALISM

Materialism is the belief that there is one substance which is matter and everything else is reducible to it, including mind.

As we have seen, modern materialism was partly made possible by the effect of **CARTESIAN DUALISM** on western thought. If matter is mere extension, and mind is non-spatial, then it is simple to bracket off mind and focus purely on the physical substance.

Arguments for materialism based on **EMPIRICAL** critiques of mind/soul/dualism:

Ryle's Philosophical Behaviourism

GILBERT RYLE calls Descartes' theory "the ghost in the machine" where **GHOST = MIND** and **MACHINE = BODY**. According to Ryle, there is no mind which exists as a separate entity to the body, and to search for one was to make a **CATEGORY MISTAKE**.

By this he means that brain and mind belong to different **LOGICAL CATEGORIES**, but have mistakenly been associated together.

One analogy for this is his story of the foreigner who, visiting Cambridge or Oxford University for the first time, is shown all the different colleges and buildings, but then asks "But where is the University?"

The mistake is that he is still looking for something separate from all the buildings he has been shown, without realising that he has already seen the university.

In just the same way, Ryle argues, dualists are mistakenly searching for something over and above the brain, or behaviour, called the mind.

Ryle was a **PHILOSOPHICAL BEHAVIOURIST** who saw "mental" events as just referring to a specific pattern of behaviour - "mind" is no longer internal; it is what we do with our bodies.

For example, when someone is depressed or angry or joyful, we look at the pattern of behaviour they exhibit in each different case and we cannot see beyond this behaviour. So **MENTAL TERMINOLOGY** actually means something physical, for example, **BEHAVIOUR**.

Evaluation

Counter-intuitive to humans as subjects who have what they perceive as internal states of mind, some of which may not manifest as outward patterns of behaviour at all - do they not exist?

Ryle partly anticipates problematic states such as wishing, which seems to have no particular pattern of behaviour attached to it, by talking about **DISPOSITIONS TO BEHAVE**.

Appropriate behaviour is regarded as potential, and can be anticipated given certain circumstances. So, a person wishing to go on holiday may spend much time on travel websites, for instance.

Ward feels Ryle's account is inadequate:

- **PRETENDING** - Firstly, what about pretending? Someone who pretends to be angry and someone who is angry may exhibit the exact same behaviour, but one of them is not experiencing the same internal state.

- **RECOGNITION** - Secondly, as mentioned, we do know our

experience from the inside, and when we feel pain for instance we know that such a feeling cannot be completely captured by a description of the way we behave when we feel it.

- **SELF-AWARE** - Thirdly, what about self-awareness? It is impossible to say how being aware of yourself as a thinking being is capable of being described in terms of behaviour or a **DISPOSITION TO BEHAVE** in a certain way.

IDENTITY THEORY

MIND-BRAIN IDENTITY is another model for the materialist explanation of **CONSCIOUSNESS**.

Although we have different words for mental events and the physical processes which underlie them, they are the same, really. For example, talk of the **EVENING STAR** and the **MORNING STAR** seems to be about two different objects - but they both refer to the same thing - the planet Venus.

Neurologists are able to point to **FMRI SCANS** which correlate some mental states with certain patterns of activity. However, it is easy to oversimplify this and many mental states involve many different parts of the brain.

Evaluation

There are clearly some key aspects of mental states that it is very difficult to explain, if they are identical to brain states.

For instance, **QUALIA** and **INTENTIONALITY**:

- **QUALIA** - These are felt experiences like smelling freshly-cut grass. They are properties of the world as seen from the subjective perspective, and cannot be seen from the "outside-looking-in"

- **INTENTIONALITY** - This describes the fact that thinking is about something, one's attention is directed towards something

Both of these properties of **CONSCIOUSNESS** seem to point to something that current materialist theories are unable to account for; after all it is hard to see how even very complex arrangements of physical "stuff" can give rise to the felt experience of tasting a hamburger.

However, Dennett says that consciousness is "a bunch of tricks in the brain", and that although it is tempting to think so, we are not experts on our own thinking, and that our minds are constantly fooling us. This means that we must be wary of assuming things like qualia cannot be explained without positing MIND.

DAWKINS ON SOUL ONE AND SOUL TWO

The biologist **RICHARD DAWKINS** has become famous for his writing on the subject of religion and science. He has said that we can discern two definitions of soul - the classical notion of soul as a non-material essence of humans, and a more modern romantic version of the soul as metaphor, a way of imaginatively experiencing the world.

The soul as metaphor:

- **SOUL AS A METAPHORICAL REALITY** - The Romantics opened up a way of understanding the soul as a metaphorical reality for the faculty which appreciates the sublime aspects of nature and existence.

- **PLATONIST DUALISTS** - However, they were influenced by Thomas Taylor's translations of Plato's works, and it is clear that many of the Romantics were essentially Platonist dualists.

- **DAWKINS** - In recent times Dawkins has called the poetic notion of soul as an **AESTHETIC SENSE** within us "soul two", which he contrasts with soul one - the traditional non-material essence.

- **SOUL TWO** - The concept of soul two, or soul as metaphor, is only soul in a weak sense, and is not a challenge or threat to a materialistic worldview.

- **ABILITY TO REACT** - Soul in this sense is just an ability to react with awe or wonder at the natural world.

- **NO PLATONIST** - So Dawkins has dropped the Platonism from the concept, and kept the poetic appreciation of the natural world.

- **NOT TWO TYPES OF SOUL** - In no sense does Dawkins believe there are two types of soul - he is using "soul one" and "soul two" as a way of showing that we should drop the classical idea of soul as non-material.

- **SCIENCE HAS KILLED SOUL ONE** - He says that science "has killed or is killing" this idea of soul.

NEED MORE HELP ON THE NATURE OF SOUL, MIND AND BODY?

Use your phone to scan this QR code

The Existence of God

Arguments about the Existence or
Non-existence of God

Arguments about the Existence or Non-existence of God

Arguments for the existence of God are part of what is known usually as Natural Theology, which is contrasted with Revealed Theology. In your Developments in Christian Theology module you will look in more detail at these. In this module we examine reasons based on sense-data, as well as reasons based on logic alone.

KEYWORDS

- **QUINQUAE VIAE** - Aquinas' Five Ways - arguments for God's existence

- **A POSTERIORI** - Describing arguments which use sense data to support their conclusion

- **ORDER** - Structure, non-chaos

- **COMPLEXITY** - Not simple, intricate or complicated

- **PURPOSE** - Goal or aim

- **EPICUREAN HYPOTHESIS** - Theory of Epicurus that given everlasting time, all possible combinations of atoms will occur

- **EVOLUTION** - Change in the heritable characteristics of biological populations over successive generations

- **COSMOLOGICAL ARGUMENT** - That the universe needs an explanation

- **NECESSITY** - The state of being required

- **PRINCIPLE OF SUFFICIENT REASON** - Principle that states that everything must have a total not partial reason

- **FALLACY OF COMPOSITION** - When one infers that something is true of the whole from the fact that it is true of some part of the whole

- **FORMAL FALLACY** - A pattern of reasoning rendered invalid by a flaw in its logical structure

- **INFORMAL FALLACY** - An invalid pattern of reasoning which is not formally fallacious

- **NECESSARY BEING** - Being which cannot not exist

- **VALID** - True by virtue of its logical form

- **ONTOLOGICAL ARGUMENT** - A priori argument for God

- **TTWNGCBC** - Acronym to help remember key part of Anselm's argument (That Than Which Nothing Greater Can Be Conceived)

- **PREDICATE** - Something which is affirmed or denied concerning an argument

ARGUMENTS BASED ON OBSERVATION

Arguments based on observation (a posteriori arguments) occupy a prominent place in the philosophy of religion. Thomas Aquinas in his Summa Theologiae set out five arguments known as the Five Ways or **QUINQUAE VIAE**. They are all a posteriori, as he did not believe an a priori argument for God would be valid. The first argument we will examine is actually the fifth of Aquinas' Five Ways.

Teleological argument (Aquinas' Fifth Way)

Teleological derives from the Greek word telos, meaning goal or purpose. The world and things in it seem to move towards certain goals or ends, so nature is viewed as directed. Teleological arguments go all the way back to Plato, who proposed that the cosmos is directed by intelligence.

Aquinas' fifth way makes use of the observation that non-intelligent organic life acts in certain ordered, cyclical and purposive ways. Eg. Acorns, given the right conditions, always grow into oak trees and not wombats; the moon has a regular 29 and a half day cycle, etc. Given that non-intelligent things such as acorns and plankton always act in certain ways for certain goals, implies that they were given those goals by an intelligence, because only intelligent beings are able to assign a purpose to things, and move that thing towards its purpose.

Aquinas gives the example of arrows fired by an archer to hit a target. Without the purposive direction imparted by the archer, the arrow would remain in the quiver. The argument relies on an Aristotelian notion of causes, especially final cause. His argument is often referred to as **QUA REGULARITY** (relating to regularity), because Aquinas is pointing to things which always occur in the same regular way to achieve the same end.

A simplified version of the argument might say that the order and purpose we see in the universe needs an explanation in terms of a guiding intelligence.

The argument can be put like this:

- The natural world obeys natural laws

- Natural things flourish as they obey these laws

- Things without intelligence can't direct themselves

- Therefore, things without intelligence require something with intelligence to direct them to their goals

- This is God

William Paley's Teleological Argument

Paley argues from order and complexity to design. His argument consists of two parts: the first is called design **QUA PURPOSE** (relating to purpose). Paley sets out an analogy in the form of a story:

- Walking across a heath, someone finding a rock would not need to ask the question as to how the rock got there - they would assume natural causes.

- But if someone found a watch on the heath, the previous answer would not work - that the watch had always been there - they would assume a designer.

- This is because of the complexity and the purpose inherent in the watch - it has been put together in a complex manner in order to tell the time - all the parts work together for that purpose, and it shows evidence of workmanship.

- If any of the parts were put together in a different way, the watch wouldn't work, which strongly implies all the parts were assembled purposefully in the right order.

- This must have been done by a designer, not by sheer chance.

Paley goes further and anticipates objections:

- Even if the watch sometimes goes wrong, this still implies it was designed for a purpose.

- We would be even more impressed with the watchmaker if the watch could produce more watches.

- Therefore, the design of the watch implies the presence of intelligence and design.

Paley goes on to look at things in the natural world which imply the evidence of design, such as the human eye, the wings of birds and the fins of fish. These are all examined in terms of design.

The second part of Paley's argument is design **QUA REGULARITY**:

- **ASTRONOMY** - He uses evidence from Astronomy, Newton's laws of motion and gravity to point to design in the universe

- **ROTATION** - He points to the regular rotation of the planets

- **DESIGN** - All of this regularity points to design

Assessing the arguments

- **BOTH ARGUMENTS** - Both arguments "beg the question". Aquinas assumes all things need a designer in order to conclude that God designed everything, Paley gives the example of a watch, something which we know has been designed, as an analogy for the world, whose design is the thing in question

- **HUME** - Analogy can only compare similar things, the watch is not similar to the universe. As the universe seems organic, why not compare something organic, like a cabbage?

- **UNIQUE UNIVERSE** - The universe is not like all the other things we can experience

- **MULTIPLE DESIGNERS** - A watch has many designers usually so, why not the universe?

- **EPICUREAN HYPOTHESIS** - The universe could have come about randomly and still look designed, given enough time, which is called the Epicurean hypothesis

- **MORAL DESIGNER** - The presence of evil and suffering in the universe prompts us to ask what kind of designer it has. For example, Dawkins' Digger Wasp

The Challenge of Evolution

There are some major challenges that Darwin's theory of evolution has thrown up against the design argument. Here are the most important:

- **RANDOM CHANGES** - These can lead to order and complex systems can be self-arranging. This is the upshot of the nature of evolution, in which organisms which adapt to their environments are able to pass on their genes more effectively than ones that can't. Thus, there is no need to appeal to a divine intelligence to account for complexity and "order". They arise "naturally" from the processes of evolution and natural selection.

- **DAWKINS & ATKINS** - Point to profound suffering and cruelty in the way the processes of evolution work. The female digger wasp for instance lays her eggs in a caterpillar so that the larva can eat the insides as they grow; she also stings it to paralyse it so it is alive as they are eating it.

- **EVOLUTION** - Challenges the Aristotelian account of causation which includes telos or purpose, as it shows that natural processes can be explained without the need to refer to a goal.

THE COSMOLOGICAL ARGUMENT

This argument is so titled because it usually refers to the **PRESENCE OF THE COSMOS AS EVIDENCE FOR GOD** - not the nature of the cosmos - that is what design arguments do. It asks the question:

"Why is there something rather than nothing?"

Aquinas' Three Ways

The classic formulations of the cosmological argument can be found in **AQUINAS' 3 WAYS**, but these have their roots in Aristotelian philosophy. In fact if you understood how and why Aristotle arrived at his Prime Mover, then you should have no problem with this argument.

▶ Aquinas' 1st Way

Objects in the Universe:

- **ARE POTENTIALLY MOVING** - All things are potentially moving. In other words, they can change into something else in the way that an acorn can change into an oak

- **MOVE FROM ONE STATE TO ANOTHER** - All things require something actual to move them from their state of potentiality. For example, a stick is potentially on fire and only becomes "actually" on fire when a flame is applied to it

- **CANNOT MOVE THEMSELVES** - From a state of potential to actual, meaning everything requires something else to move it, but you must have a first mover which is not moved itself to be the cause of the movement of other things (if you did not, there would be no explanation for the movement of the things which are currently in motion, because you cannot keep going back forever in the chain of movement)

- **REQUIRE A FIRST MOVER** - This first mover which imparts motion to other things but which is not moved is called God

▶ Aquinas 2nd Way

Objects in the Universe:

- **SELF-PERPETUATE** - All things are caused by other things

- **CANNOT REPRODUCE ALONE** - Nothing can be the cause of itself

- **REQUIRE AN INITIAL CAUSE** - You cannot keep going back in the series of causes forever, or you would have no things now. In other words, if there was no initial cause, there could not be other causes. There must be a first cause, itself uncaused, which began the causes

- **ARE CAUSED BY GOD** - This is what people call God

▶ Aquinas' 3rd Way

Objects in the Universe:

- **ARE CONTINGENT** - All things can possibly not exist

- **CAME FROM NOTHING** - If time is infinite, there must have been a point when there was nothing

- **WOULD STILL BE NOTHING** - If there was nothing once, there would be nothing now

- **REQUIRED SOMETHING** - There must be something that is necessary (impossible not to exist)

- **WERE NECESSARY** - Everything that is necessary is either caused by another necessary thing or not

- **ARE UNIQUE** - You cannot have an infinite series of such causes

- **WERE CAUSED BY NECESSITY** - There must be an uncaused necessary being

- **ARE CAUSED BY GOD** - This is what people call God

HUME'S CRITICISMS OF ARGUMENTS FROM OBSERVATION

What Does David Hume Say?

- **NO EXPERIENCE** - We have no experience of universes being made, so we cannot claim to know what caused this one

- **INFINITE REGRESS** - It may be that an infinite regress is possible - see oscillating universe hypothesis

- **UNIVERSE NECESSARY** - It may be that the universe itself is necessary

- **WHY ASSUME?** - Why assume that the necessary thing is a being, or even a being called God?

Teleological Argument

- **POOR ANALOGY** - Analogies are stronger the more alike the two things being compared are. In the case of the design argument Hume claims that the world and the watch are very unlike each other. The world is composed of organic and mineral matter, so it is not like a machine, and more like an organism.

- **MANY GOVERNING PRINCIPLES** - Hume says that the governing principle of the world could be one of many such as generation or gravity, and that these would work equally as well as intelligence. There might not even be one supreme governing principle, but many, each in charge of their own domain.

- **BEGS THE QUESTION** - The analogy of a man-made thing is bound to lead to the conclusion that the universe was designed, but Hume points out that we already have experience or knowledge of watches or houses being made, and so this just begs the question when it comes to the universe.

- **ANTHROPOMORPHISM** - Also, the analogy of a man-made thing implies a human-like God (like effects imply like causes), but this causes problems as God is meant to be infinite in His qualities: A perfect God cannot be inferred from the state of the universe; as Hume says:

"The world is very faulty and imperfect, and was only the first rude essay of some infant deity who abandoned it"

- **MORALITY** - Analogy leads to a non-moral God. One should judge the craftsman on the quality of the work they produce. Earthquakes and illness do not imply a just God. There could be two gods or forces, a good and an evil. That would explain far better the state of the universe.

Cosmological Argument

Hume attacks the principle of **SUFFICIENT REASON** on which the 3rd Way is founded. This principle states that there should be a total explanation rather than a partial one for any phenomenon. Hume argues that you cannot move from saying individual elements of the universe require an explanation, to the whole universe requiring an explanation. This is to commit the **FALLACY OF COMPOSITION**. The fallacy of composition is to assume that just because all the individual members of a group of things have a certain property, that the group itself will have that property. For instance, just because all the tiles on a floor are square, does not mean that the whole floor has to be square - it could be many other shapes.

However, the fallacy of composition is not a **FORMAL FALLACY** and does not always hold: If you substitute colour for shape in the floor tile example above, it is clear that the fallacy doesn't work (if every floor tile is red, then the whole floor **WILL** be red).

So the question is whether contingency is a property more like shape or colour in the floor tile analogy. It certainly seems difficult to see how if everything in the universe is dependent on other things for its existence, how the universe as a whole could not also be dependent on something else for its existence.

Hume questions the **REALITY OF THE WHOLE** that people refer to, saying that "whole" things are usually created by "arbitrary acts of the mind". Eg. when we unite several counties into one kingdom, this has no influence on the nature of things, it is simply a human perception.

The word **UNIVERSE** could be just a convenient term for our own perceptions, rather than referring to any reality. Modern physics would seem to provide some support for this with the view of **POCKET UNIVERSES** that exist within larger ones - to look for a "whole" gets very difficult in this view.

Hume says that it is not inconceivable that the world had no cause, or just always existed. He says "it is neither intuitively or demonstratively certain" that every object that begins to exist owes its existence to a cause.

He also says that **LIKE CAUSES PRODUCE LIKE EFFECTS**. This seems to be true in the case of parent rabbits producing baby rabbits, for example, so as many things in the universe seem to be the offspring of two parents, why should we assume that there is one male "parent" of the universe. Wouldn't it make more sense to postulate a male and female creator God?

To base an argument on causation would be foolish, as we could never be sure that causation is anything other than a psychological effect. In fact it would be even more foolish in the case of the universe, because lacking past experience of formation of universes, we haven't even got anything to base our "habit of mind" on.

Any being that exists can also not exist, and there is **NO CONTRADICTION** implied in conceiving its non-existence, but this is exactly what would have to be the case, if its existence were necessary. So the term **NECESSARY BEING** makes no sense a posteriori. Any being claimed to exist may or may not exist. In Hume's own words "All existential propositions are synthetic."

ARGUMENTS BASED ON REASON

Arguments based on reason are **VALID A PRIORI**, without the need to refer to observations from experience; they are simply logically true in the same way that the argument:

All men are mortal ➜ Socrates is a man ➜ Therefore Socrates is mortal

Is logically true. A priori arguments are true by definition, in the same way that 2+2=4 is true by definition because another way of defining 2+2 is to call it 4. If it can be shown that God exists by definition then a priori arguments would work.

▸ The Ontological Argument

The argument is known in different forms. The generally accepted classical formulation is from Anselm (1033-1109). It is found in chapters 2-4 of his work Proslogion . The logical demonstration in the argument either totally succeeds or totally fails - it is a **LOGICAL DEDUCTIVE ARGUMENT**.

▸ Anselm's Argument (1st form)

God is that than which nothing greater can be conceived - **TTWNGCBC**.

Even the atheist can have this definition in his understanding.

But if he has it in his understanding (ie in the mind) only, then there must be a greater being who exists both in the mind and reality (it is greater to exist both in the mind and reality).

Therefore, by the definition **TTWNGCBC**, God must exist both in the mind and in reality.

Another way of saying this is that it is self-contradictory to be capable of conceiving something than which nothing greater can be thought, and at the same time to deny that that something really exists.

▸ Anselm's Argument (2nd form)

The second form of the argument is developed to show the impossibility of conceiving of God as not existing. God cannot not be. Any lesser form of existence where it was possible not to be, would not fit with the definition of God:

- God is **TTWNGCBC** (see 1st form)

- It is greater to be a necessary being than a contingent being

- If God exists only contingently it would be possible to imagine a greater being who exists necessarily

- But if God is **TTWNGCBC** then that being has to be God

- God therefore must be a necessary being, and exist in reality

It is important to note that this is logical necessity and not factual necessity (the kind of necessity arrived at in the cosmological argument).

Evaluation

▸ Gaunilo

A monk, contemporary of Anselm argued you could not define things into existence.

Constructed a reductio ad absurdum argument to show the flaw in Anselm's argument:

- Imagine a lost island - the most excellent of all islands

- You can form the idea of this island in your mind

- Therefore, according to Anselm's logic the island must exist in reality

- But this is absurd, and so is Anselm's argument

Anselm replied that islands are contingent things and therefore do not have necessary existence, whereas God does.

▸ Kant

- Kant argued that "It would be self-contradictory to posit a triangle and yet reject its three angles, but there is no contradiction in rejecting the triangle together with its three angles

- In other words, if God exists he must be necessary, but only if. Definitions can only tell us what God would be like if he existed

- Kant says that existence is not a real predicate. It does not give us any information about an object. 'to exist' merely means that an object is actual

- Existence adds nothing to a concept:

   "If we take the subject (God) with all its predicates (eg. all knowledge), and say "God is" or "There is a God", we attach no new predicate to the concept of God ... merely posit it as being an object that stands in relation to my concept. The content of both must be one and the same ... The real contains no more than the merely possible. A hundred real thalers (German coins) do not contain the least coin more than a hundred possible thalers."

NEED MORE HELP ON ARGUMENTS ABOUT THE EXISTENCE AND NON-EXISTENCE OF GOD?

Use your phone to scan this QR code

God and the World

Religious Experience

The Problem of Evil and Suffering

Religious Experience

What is religious experience? Many people claim to have directly or indirectly experienced God in some way. Research by Alister Hardy has shown that between 25-45% of adults have had an experience of a presence or power beyond themselves.

RICHARD SWINBURNE has given a schema to fit the different kinds of religious experience into, as they vary considerably. A person can seem to perceive God:

- In experiencing a normal non-religious object, for instance, a sunset

- In experiencing an unusual public object, eg. Jesus' resurrection appearances

(these are public)

- In private sensations describable in normal language (eg. Jacob's ladder dream)

- In private sensations not describable in normal language (eg. mystical experiences)

- Without any sensations, but seeing the whole course of experience in the light of God, or being unable to point to any particular thing that made them seem to be experiencing God

(these three are private)

KEYWORDS

- **RELIGIOUS EXPERIENCE** - An experience of a presence or power beyond oneself

- **EXTROVERTIVE EXPERIENCE** - Stace's term for a **PANTHEISTIC** religious experience

- **INTROVERTIVE EXPERIENCE** - Stace's term for a religious experience in which one's sense of self is dissolved in a greater reality

- **THEISTIC** - Related to a personal, loving creator God

- **MONISTIC** - Related to an impersonal divine ultimate, such as Brahman

- **INEFFABLE** - Indescribable in normal language

- **PASSIVE** - James' term for the experience of loss of control during a religious experience

- **NOETIC** - Bestowing insight or wisdom beyond rational understanding

- **TRANSIENT** - Fleeting, over in a short space of time

- **NUMINOUS** - Otto's term for a powerful and awe-inspiring experience of the divine as "other"

- **MYSTERIUM TREMENDUM** - Otto's term for the nature of the numinous experience - a mystery experienced as overwhelming

- **CREATURE-FEELING** - The feeling of being a contingent, created being, brought on by a numinous experience

- **CONVERSION** - A turning-away from past sinful life, and beginning anew with inner certainty of faith

- **REPENTANCE** - Experiencing remorse for one's sins, saying sorry for them

- **METANOIA** - Literally "changing one's mind", a change of heart resulting in changed way of life

- **VERIDICAL** - Truthful in the sense of relating to a real state of affairs

- **PRINCIPLE OF RATIONALITY** - A fundamental assumption of reasoning, without which no such reasoning would be possible

- **PHYSIOLOGICAL** - Relating to the physical body

- **PSYCHOLOGICAL** - Relating to the mind or psyche

- **ASCETIC** - Relating to the strict practices such as fasting which religious people often undertake

MYSTICAL EXPERIENCE

This has been characterised in different ways. It is usually seen as difficult to put into ordinary language. However, some qualities such as an apprehension of ultimate reality, or an experience of the living God, are often used. The experiences often accompanied by feelings of bliss, deep and lasting joy, humility, transformative effect on one's behaviour and relations with others.

Some attempts to classify mystical experiences:

W T Stace

- **EXTROVERTIVE MYSTICAL EXPERIENCES** - The plurality of objects in the world are transfigured into a single living entity

- **INTROVERTIVE MYSTICAL EXPERIENCES** - A loss of identity as a separate individual occurs, and one merges into the divine reality

R C Zaehner

- **THEISTIC MYSTICISM** - Awareness of God in a living relationship

- **MONISTIC MYSTICISM** - Awareness of the soul, Self or consciousness

William James' characteristics of a mystical experience

- **INEFFABLE** - Impossible to put into words

- **NOETIC** - Conveying insights into the nature of reality which transcend normal discursive thought

- **TRANSIENT** - Fleeting, over within a short space of time

- **PASSIVE** - The mystic feels unable to control the experience, feels "taken over" by it

Rudolf Otto

In **THE IDEA OF THE HOLY**, Otto outlines a concept which he calls the **NUMINOUS**. This approach to mystical experience is one which emphasises God's separateness and otherness. Numinous comes from the latin numen, meaning divinity. Otto was trying to convey by it the original sense of awe-inspiring wonder and terror which he believed lay at the heart of religious experience.

One example is the fear that the disciples felt when Jesus calmed the storm, a supernatural fear, contrasted with their fear of the storm itself, it was a far more profound fear. Another example might be this from Isaiah 6: 1-5:

> "*I saw the Lord, high and exalted, seated on a throne; and the train of his robe filled the temple. Above him were seraphim, each with six wings: With two wings they covered their faces, with two they covered their feet, and with two they were flying. ₃And they were calling to one another:*
>
> *'Holy, holy, holy is the Lord Almighty*
>
> *the whole earth is full of his glory.'*
>
> *At the sound of their voices the doorposts and thresholds shook and the temple was filled with smoke.*
>
> *'Woe to me!' I cried. 'I am ruined! For I am a man of unclean lips, and I live among a people of unclean lips, and my eyes have seen the King, the Lord Almighty.'*"

The characteristic of this experience is the feeling of utter worthlessness, helplessness and dependence experienced by the prophet upon seeing the Lord God.

Otto uses two other latin words to explain the numinous:

- **MYSTERIUM** - The experience is in some sense unavailable to ordinary human reason. It is a mystery. Otto wanted to remind us of the "mystery schools" of Ancient Greece, in which neophytes would undergo rituals involving being led into darkness and being forbidden to speak about the initiation.

- **TREMENDUM** - The experience is awe-inspiring, and both attracts us, and makes us feel our own inferiority as mere creatures. Following from this is:

- **CREATURE-FEELING** - Related to the above characteristic, a sense of one's own contingency as a created being in relation to the source of that existence

EXAMPLES OF MYSTICAL EXPERIENCE

St. Teresa of Avila

In The Interior Castle she outlines many types of religious experience. Through mental prayer:

"God gave her spiritual delights: the prayer of quiet where God's presence overwhelmed her senses, raptures where God overcame her with glorious foolishness, prayer of union where she felt the sun of God melt her soul away."

Jan Van Ruusbroec

"There follows the union without distinction. Enlightened men have found themselves an essential contemplation which is above and beyond reason, and a fruitive tendency which pierces through every condition and all being, and in which they immerse themselves in a wayless abyss of fathomless beatitude where the Trinity of the Divine Persons possess their nature in essential unity."

Conversion experience

Conversion – turning-towards – is a term usually used to describe the process of someone turning away from past sinful behaviour, and beginning a new life based on faith in God. Repentance, the word used in the Gospels to describe the action of leaving sin behind and beginning a new life in Christ, is translated from a Greek word metanoia, which has the sense of a turning away from sin, a complete and fundamental change of heart. Conversion is thus a foundational element of Christian life. It can be gradual or sudden, but most practising Christians have some experience of it.

Radical examples of conversion can be found in St. Paul and John Wesley:

- **ST PAUL** - Originally called Saul, Paul was a Jew who persecuted Christians until a sudden experience of the risen Christ on the road to Damascus. He described himself as a new man, a new creation.

- **JOHN WESLEY** - Initially aware that he did not have the same faith in a personal saviour that he saw others had, he had a conversion experience in which he felt his heart warmed and felt trust in Christ that he had been saved from his sins.

WILLIAM JAMES examines conversion in the light of his psychological account of the **SICK SOUL** and the "healthy-minded soul". The sick soul is a personality type that is depressive and pessimistic; the healthy-minded soul is conversely optimistic about life. James claims that whilst it can occur to both types, conversion affects the sick soul in a more profound and long-lasting way. We will examine some key claims of James regarding the sick and healthy-minded soul.

THE HEALTHY-MINDED SOUL AND THE SICK SOUL

"The completest religions would therefore seem to be those in which the pessimistic elements are best developed. Buddhism, of course, and Christianity are the best known to us of these. They are essentially religions of deliverance: the man must die to an unreal life before he can be born into the real life."

William James, Varieties of Religious Experience, Lecture 7

Here are the essentials of James' views on the sick soul and conversion. He begins by delineating the healthy-minded attitude to evil. He claims that this is really to minimise the power of evil, and try to evade it. This makes them happier and more well-adjusted than the sick soul, who tends to dwell on and be affected by evil.

James sees certain types of Christianity as more amenable to the healthy-minded view. For instance, in the Catholic sacrament of confession, one can confess one's sins and "walk away from them" in James' words. He contrasts the healthy-minded view with the more pessimistic view of the sick soul, quoting Goethe who said looking back on his life he had found it "nothing but pain and burden". James believed that when faced with the all-embracing blackness of death, the healthy-minded attitude had nothing to offer, and that the sick soul could have a more profound experience of living.

The Once-Born and the Twice-Born

Using this hierarchy, James makes a further distinction between the once-born and twice-born. The former correspond with the healthy-minded soul, and the latter with the sick soul. For example, the Greek religion, almost entirely naturalistic, corresponds with the healthy-minded soul, but he claims that the Epicureans and Stoics (Greeks) knew no joys like those religions of the twice-born such as Buddhism and Christianity, in which a process of dying and rising happens psychologically to the believer.

EVALUATION

How should we understand religious experience?

Religious experience can be understood in at least three different ways:

- **UNION** - Firstly, as union with a greater power

- **PSYCHOLOGICAL** - Secondly as a psychological effect such as an illusion

- **PHYSIOLOGICAL** - Thirdly as the product of a physiological effect

Union with a greater power

This would mean the experience was veridical, and therefore does not merely seem to be an experience of God, but actually is an experience of God. The problem is that as the experience is merely subjective and private, how can the person who has it be certain of this?

SWINBURNE formulated his principle of credulity to answer this question.

The principle states that we ought to believe that things are as they seem to be unless we have evidence that we are mistaken. This is an axiomatic principle of rationality which we apply all the time without even considering it in everyday life. Swinburne says:

> *"If you say the contrary - never trust appearances until it is proved that they are reliable - you will never have any beliefs at all. For what would show that appearances are reliable, except more appearances? And, if you cannot trust appearances as such, you cannot trust these new ones either. Just as you must trust your five ordinary senses, so it is equally rational to trust your religious sense."*

So Swinburne's method is the clever one of asking why we make an exception to an axiomatic principle of rationality when it comes to religion.

WILLIAM JAMES also argued for an openness to this sort of interpretation. Using a psychological approach and gathering a large range of testimonies he argued for a **COMMON CORE** to religious experience (see above). His conclusions were:

- **VISIBLE WORLD** - That the visible world is part of a more spiritual universe from which it draws its chief significance

- **TRUE END** - That union or harmonious relation with that higher universe is our true end

- **PRAYER** - That prayer or inner communion with the spirit thereof, be that spirit "God" or "law", is a process wherein work is really done, and spiritual energy flows in and produces effects, psychological or material, within the phenomenal world.

Religion includes also the following **PSYCHOLOGICAL CHARACTERISTICS**:

- **A NEW ZEST** - Which adds itself like a gift to life, and takes the form either of lyrical enchantment or of appeal to earnestness and heroism

- **AN ASSURANCE OF SAFETY** - And a temper of peace, and, in relation to others, a preponderance of loving affections

Mackie says of James:

"Even what he classes as genuinely religious experiences (ones which leave 'good dispositions' in the believer) do not intrinsically resist explanation in purely human terms."

Others such as Dawkins have argued similarly: psychological or physiological explanations are far more likely given the prior improbability of a divine being who interacts with humans.

Psychological effect such as an illusion

Often experiences can deceive us, eg. hallucinations. Some people may be mistaken, and even self-deluding.

Freud thought that we feel helpless, need a father figure and create one unconsciously with religious experience, which helps us satisfy the need for security. Jung believed that archetypes in the collective unconscious can cause religious experience.Just because some people are mistaken or hallucinate, it doesn't mean all religious experience is of this character.

And, just because God appears as a father in the way we need Him, doesn't prove that religious experience is not true. It may be God appears that way because he has placed that deep need in us.

Physiological effects

There are well-documented links between the body and the mind. There are **PSYCHOSOMATIC** factors in some illnesses, such as psoriasis and high blood pressure. And the mind can affect things like heart rate, feelings of nausea and so on. As many religious experiences can be subtle, feeling-based, it is possible that physiological factors may be a major cause. Some possible causes include:

- **ASCETIC** - Practices such as fasting can lead to hallucinations etc.
- **PERSINGER HELMET** - This shows how manipulating magnetic fields in the brain can give rise to feelings of a "presence".

- **LIMITED UNDERSTANDING** - We still have a very limited understanding of how the brain works and interacts with physical processes in other parts of the body - it is possible that we will understand religious experiences in natural terms when our knowledge grows.

NEED MORE HELP ON RELIGIOUS EXPERIENCE?

Use your phone to scan this QR code

The Problem of Evil and Suffering

The problem of evil has occupied the thought of theologians for centuries. Many religions and mythologies attempt to account for the existence of evil and suffering in the world - often, as in dualistic worldviews, good and evil gods are at war with each other and this explains the state of the world, split between moments of good and evil, but with neither force ever attaining final triumph. With the advent of monotheism in the revelation to the Israelites a new problem arises. God is the supreme, all-powerful and all-loving God of the universe, and therefore if creation is good, as the Genesis texts say it is, then the existence of evil creates a unique problem. That problem is set out in its two main forms below.

KEYWORDS

- **OMNIPOTENT** - All-powerful

- **LOGICAL PROBLEM** - Description of the problem of evil relating to the coherence of God's attributes and the evil in the world

- **EVIDENTIAL PROBLEM** - Version of the problem of evil relating to sheer amount of evil in the world

- **INDUCTIVE** - Describing the process of induction

- **INSCRUTABILITY** - Unfathomable or unknowable nature of God

- **THEODICY** - Defence of God

- **PRIVATION** - Lack of something which should be possessed by nature

- **EXITUS/REDITUS** - "Going out and coming back"

- **SOUL-MAKING** - Type of theodicy in which suffering leads to growth

- **UNIVERSALISM** - Belief that all will be saved

DIFFERENT VERSIONS OF THE PROBLEM

Logical problem

The logical problem of evil highlights the inconsistency between divine attributes and the presence of evil. It is usually put in the form below.

The **INCONSISTENT TRIAD**. First stated by **EPICURUS**, this dilemma can be put like this:

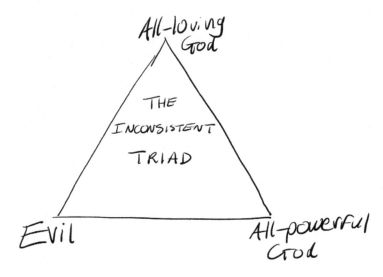

Either God cannot abolish evil, or he will not; if he cannot then he is not all-powerful; if he will not then he is not all-good

The logical form of this can be stated:

- God is **OMNIPOTENT**

- God is **ALL-GOOD**

- God **OPPOSES EVIL**

- Therefore **EVIL DOES NOT EXIST**

Clearly, the conclusion is problematic. Most people would disagree with it. If you disagree with the conclusion, then at least one of the premises must be false.

To deny any of the premises is to deny the God of classical theism:

- **GOD IS OMNIPOTENT** - If you say that He is not all-powerful then you are saying there are things God cannot do. This sounds like it cedes too much ground to the challenge, but most theologians would argue that God's omnipotence is not completely unlimited. In other words, God is not free to do the logically impossible, such as create a square circle, or do an evil act (Aquinas argues that God cannot do this because this would create a lack in God, but as God is perfect he cannot lack any good).

- **NON-INTERFERENCE** - Some would also include God's inability to interfere with human free-will as a self-imposed limitation of God, as part of his loving nature. This is one partial solution to the problem of evil, as we shall see later.

- **GOD IS ALL-GOOD** - This premise is more difficult to get around. If God is not all-good, then we have some mixture of good and evil in God which the main monotheistic religions would deny.

- **GOD OPPOSES EVIL** - God clearly opposes evil, but it might be worth asking in the long-term whether God might allow certain evils to bring about even greater goods. This has also been vigorously debated. See Dostoevsky - The Grand Inquisitor in The Brothers Karamazov for an examination of this question.

The evidential problem of evil

The problem of suffering emphasises a different aspect of the problem of evil. The focus is on the experience of evil, the intensity, and the amount of it. The evidence of so much evil in the world is indeed difficult to explain for the theist.

Whilst arguments from the logical problem of evil aim to show that God's existence is impossible, evidential arguments have the more modest aim of showing that God's existence is unlikely.

Evidential arguments are inductive, in that they point to particular cases of evil in the world.

Most responses to the evidential problem refer to the inscrutability of God's action, and aim to show that God could be justified in allowing the existence of radical evil.

THEODICIES

Augustine

Augustine's use of original perfection and the Fall to justify evil is the classic defence of God or theodicy. It can be presented in steps:

- God is good and made a flawless world "ex-nihilo". (Genesis 1)

- Humans (and angels) were created with free will

- Evil is created when this free will is used to turn from God to a lesser good

- Evil is "not a substance", but a "privation of good"

- Natural evil is deserved suffering in response to Adam's sin

- Moral evil was the cause of natural evil. Natural evil is a disorder introduced into God's ordered world

Augustine believes that sin is an **ONTOLOGICAL CONDITION** - something that human nature is marked with from the choice of free created beings - angels and humans. The possibility of turning from greater to lesser goods is there in the world both because of free will , and in the way that the world was created by God, in a hierarchical fashion. Some things are better and more valuable than others. Clearly, the theodicy relies on free will: criticisms of it often focus on this and question whether free will can take the weight that Augustine places on it.

Evaluation of Augustine

Modern science rejects the idea of an original perfect state from which we fell. Evolution emphasises the way in which organisms develop from cruder to more complex systems – applied to culture and humanity and morality it implies progress means we are moving away from an original amoral state to an enlightened one. This is clearly highly debatable and many call this the **MYTH OF PROGRESS**.

It seems strange in the modern era to view sin as transferred in a hereditary fashion. Some view this as an outdated idea based on a misunderstanding of biology. For instance, Augustine's claim that we were "all in Adam's loins" reveals a belief that all of the human race was present as seed in Adam's loins and therefore, that all are corrupted by his sin. Needless to say there are many who disagree with such a literal version of the transmission of original sin:

- **PERFECTION** - If humans were created perfect why did they desire to sin? If they did desire to sin, surely that shows they were not created perfect? Couldn't God have created a world where people didn't sin even though they had the possibility of doing so?

- **RESPONSIBILITY** - If God foresaw the evil that would befall and planned to send Christ to redeem the world doesn't that imply some responsibility for evil on God's part?

- **DEBATABLE** - Evil as a privation is debatable and some evil might be characterised as a lack, other evil as an actual presence

- **INCOMPATIBLE** - Augustine's theodicy involves an eternal hell, which seems incompatible with an all-loving God

Is it logically possible for a perfect world to go wrong, and if it is, isn't that ultimately the responsibility of the creator of that world?

Some defences of Augustine

- **MYTHOLOGY** - There is just as much mythologizing involved in placing a "golden age" in the future, as there is in the past. Some would argue that moderns have simply swapped one myth for another.

- **ASPECT OF CUNNING** - Some readings of Genesis interpret the serpent as an aspect of created humanity which is crafty or cunning. In other words, using a gift of God in a way that is less than it is meant to do, to glorify self rather than God and others. This means it is not that God put evil desires in us, rather that freedom means we can choose how to employ our gifts. When we began to systematically employ them in selfish ways, we separated ourselves from God.

- **FREE LOVE** - Love between God and his creatures is only possible if they are free – this means that without freedom we could not share in God's love. Theologians characterise the great gift-giving love of God as **EXITUS AND REDITUS**: a going-out and a returning. Human free will is involved in that return to God, we get to participate in the divine life, which is the flourishing of true freedom.

The Irenaean Theodicy

Found in the writings of **IRENAEUS** (130-202). It is a soul-making theodicy, in that it emphasises the importance of evil and suffering in helping us to develop specific qualities of soul. Evil and suffering therefore play an important role in our salvation. JOHN HICK has developed it in recent times.

GEN 1:26 - Distinguishes between the image and likeness of God. Humans are created in the image of God (ie. they have free will, know good from evil, are capable of rational and moral action and love), but must grow into the likeness of God (actually perform loving actions, choose good and not evil, use free will in the best way), and the only way that this is possible is in a world in which it is significantly possible to turn away from the good. This world is called by **HICK** a **VALE OF SOUL-MAKING** for this reason.

"Then God said, 'Let us make mankind in our image, in our likeness, so that they may rule over the fish in the sea and the birds in the sky, over the livestock and all the wild animals, and over all the creatures that move along the ground'. So God created mankind in his own image, in the image of God he created them; male and female he created them."

Gen 1:26-28

There are therefore two stages which make up the development of humanity:

- **IMAGE OF GOD** - The appearance of humans as the culmination of the evolutionary process

- **MORAL AWARENESS** - The second stage (corresponding to the 'likeness of God') is the dawning of moral awareness in humans and their seeking through religion to love God and neighbour

The **FALL OF HUMANITY** is a failure within this second phase. It is an inevitable part of the maturation process – it helps people to grow and develop.

Hick said the value of this world is:

"To be judged, not primarily by the quantity of pleasure and pain occurring in it at any particular moment, but by its fitness for its primary purpose, the purpose of soul-making."

He argues that God creates people at an **EPISTEMIC DISTANCE** (a distance in knowledge of God) so that they are not compelled to know Him, but must choose to come to know him through an act of faith.

Also, if we do not complete our journey to the likeness of God in this life, we must complete it in the next - but God **GUARANTEES OUR ULTIMATE SALVATION**.

Evaluation of the Irenaean Theodicy

- **UNIVERSAL SALVATION** - This theory is called **UNIVERSALISM**. Some condemn it as unscriptural, and doing away with the need to be moral altogether

- **AUSCHWITZ** - How does suffering like that at Auschwitz justify the **SOUL-MAKING** of individuals? Surely this suffering broke humans rather than perfected them?

- **DYSTELEOLOGICAL EVIL** - Linked to this is the problem of Dysteleological evil - evil that has no purpose. Again the "protest atheism" of Ivan Karamazov which wants no part in God's plan: "I must return my ticket"

- **LEVEL OF SUFFERING** - Do we need such a large amount of suffering to help us develop – gratuitous evil and suffering are a problem for this theodicy

- **WHY PERFECTION?** - Why does God need to use such a long painful process of evolution to perfect humans?

- **OPPORTUNITY** - The theodicy is in keeping with Christian understandings of suffering – that it can be used as an opportunity rather than a limitation. For example, Job

NEED MORE HELP ON THE PROBLEM OF EVIL AND SUFFERING?

Use your phone to scan this QR code

Lightning Source UK Ltd.
Milton Keynes UK
UKOW01f0811301017
311871UK00015B/967/P